The
Infinite
Town

By the same author

Rigmarole
The Domesticity Remix
The Horse Burning Park
Half A Mind
Gaps Between Hills (with Andy Croft and Dermot Blackburn)
How I Learned to Sing: New and Selected Poems
6 Degrees of Connection: Towards the Absolute Alrightness of the Kids

Words Out Loud: 10 Essays on the Poetry Reading (editor)

Tactics for the Tightrope: Creative Resilience for Creative Communities

The Infinite Town

Mark Robinson

Smokestack Books
School Farm
Nether Silton
North Yorkshire
YO7 2JZ.
e-mail: info@smokestack-books.co.uk
www.smokestack-books.co.uk

Poems copyright
Mark Robinson, 2024,
all rights reserved.

ISBN 9781739173081

Smokestack Books
is represented by
Inpress Ltd

for Joe

'At this time of life whatever being there is is doing a lot of listening'
John Ashbery

'Continental islands are accidental, derived islands. They are separated from a continent, born of disarticulation, erosion, fracture; they survive the absorption of what once contained them. Oceanic islands are originary, essential islands. Some are formed from coral reefs and display a genuine organism. Others emerge from underwater eruptions, bringing to the light of day a movement from the lowest depths. Some rise slowly; some disappear and then return, leaving us no time to annex them. These two kinds of islands, continental and originary, reveal a profound opposition between ocean and land. Continental islands serve as a reminder that the sea is on top of the earth, taking advantage of the slightest sagging in the highest structures; oceanic islands, that the earth is still there, under the sea, gathering its strength to punch through to the surface.'

Gilles Deleuze

Contents

Full Title Guarantee   9

The Infinite Town
The Infinite Town   13
From the Proverbs of Aurora Boroborealis   14
Autumn   15
The disappearing men   16
Hindsight   17
Early, Near the Courts   19
Freeport   20
They talk only about last night, what they did and   21
All communities are imagined communities: 22
New Year's Eve   23
Water   24
Policy Announcement   25
Technique   27
Anniversary Aubade   29

Homewards
Misunderstandings   33
The Minister is Dreaming in the Sun   34
Freedom   35
Borders   36
Festival   38
Homewards   41
And if we do not meet again   42
For Some People in a House Without Walls   43
They think they are the serious ones but   44
The Present Imperfect   45
If We Look Back   46
Moving the Books   48

A Confession
Born backwards, October 1964   51
1970   52
'Kin Errors: 53
Self-portrait discovered while playing with two
    triangles by Guillevic   55
DNA tells me   56
The mice in the attic   57
A Confession   58
Tasting Menu   59
My father died a year ago today   66
Attempting to leave   70
In a different light   71
Some days   73
A message from the recently dead   74
Epithalamium for Cineastes   75

Recursion
Recursion: a mobile rendered in two dimensions   79

Notes and acknowledgements   91

Full Title Guarantee

These poems are now private property.
They may be accessed only with permission
of The Infinite Corporation,
who have full title guarantee until
Universal Darkness buries all.

These lines have been remediated
for contaminant-free development
with the use of public investment.
The costs of such enabling works
shall be considered immaterial to
future sales of these poems or derivatives,
and to any rent charged thereupon.

The Infinite Corporation have acquired
these poems for a proportionate fee,
a share of future uncapitalised revenues
and unlimited future investment.
As policy, The Corporation denies
all Freedom of Information requests.

Access to this book may be withdrawn
if it is copied or used inappropriately.
Access to the white space between stanzas
and to all punctuation is offered freely
as per the pertinent Section 106 agreement.

The transfer of these lines is now absolute and complete.
The Infinite Corporation covenant to cover
costs of upkeep, improvement and repair,
subject to proportionate and infinite charges.

The Infinite Corporation reserves the right to
dispose of these lines as it sees fit.

The Infinite Town

'Of the world, weather-swept, with which one shares the century'

George Oppen

The Infinite Town

A slice of future
Has tracked us down
The river's freshness
The afterflash of fireworked skies

These stones listen
To the infinite town
In the rasp of morning
The slow breath of dusk

A hope
That now and here
May be somewhere to settle
And train ourselves to dream

From the Proverbs of Auroro Boroborealis

Walk with me. Aurora Boroborealis is my name.
My wisdom's cast from flare stack flames.

Dim the glow of town and works, embrace the dark:
Laughter rockets out a molten spark.

Clear skies present a bouquet of glories:
Tonight will be one of your happier stories.

Learn the patterns of the sky and tomorrow's sunshine.
The sharing of a bad photo will bring on rain.

How far up, the brightness we dream, how far away:
Life a dash and a push through a field of waves.

When you and the universe exhale together,
Past, present and future meet where there is no weather.

Tonight's a singing net of colours to walk you home,
Let the sister of sun and moon mend your cracked hopes with gold.

Autumn

Flat real forever feels like a dream.
Everything is shrinking.
Husk houses now in fields crackle white.
Their bricks flake beneath wind.
Soon this all comes as default.

Every street and couple the same frayed edges.

Breaking light a stripe on the horizon.
A dog shadows its own breathless dance.
Only changeless air moving, golden.
And then repetition, re-education, a start.
The autumn news dons its mask.

The disappearing men

are folding themselves into
the corners of their silences.
They gaze from clifftops
while no one watches them,
contemplate the sea's due care.
They hold their breath.

They are in the middle of
the flyover, seemingly stuck,
but not really, not really, they just
bide their time, do not look into
the lorries, want the driver's
catastrophe to be random.

In the shadow of the questions
that never came, the broken branches
the dog walkers will find, they lay
down their burdens, they weigh
down those things that must
be weighed down before they are lost.

They head gracefully towards
the shush of the splash, somewhere
quiet, where the moment is whole.
They dream their way onto the tracks,
walk the parallel lines which meet
only at the vanishing point.

You could easily miss them,
not suppose they were ever there,
be unsure what it was you saw,
not believe the size of the crowds
that welcome them as they arrive,
as they disappear.

Hindsight

Known only to the crane, the drone
and the pilot hunting a soft landing
right by its furthest reach,
a place never touched or left alone,
further and dustier than a star,
every rainbow is secretly a circle,
were we far enough away to see.

The bow from which the arrow flies,
that joins the dots and worlds
and bridges night and day,
ourselves and those we've yet to join,
is one step from perfect, always
bending towards something better,
were we far enough away to see.

The long arc is slow but makes rain stop.
We cannot touch the possibilities,
each star already cracked to let life in,
its blues and golds and greens
dimmed to orange then red to cool
colour into tonight, and tomorrow,
were we far enough away to see.

Where the rainbow ends the land forms.
Villages, towns, cities, worlds grow,
families, gangs, bands and fellowships,
all the polyphonic shapes of identity
assume their place in the dance,
to shift from flat earth's rhythm,
were we far enough away to see.

Your night's colours overlap mine,
even as we stand side by side.
They shift with the angle of our tears,
the way the moonlight bounces
off the ghosts in the curves of our faces,
and their gestures, their waves,
were we far enough away to see.

This year the rainbows twinned in glory
triplet branches into every corner,
set muted hues to hunt in shadows
till we can bear to look no longer.
And then the moon comes out, fresh
as milk, as snow on a bin-lid,
were we far enough away to see.

And all the colours are a little harder
to pin down as they stream towards us,
a rainbow caught only with luck,
bright, bold, playful, nameless and full
of what the naked eye knows only as love,
falling at the right angle, to a backdrop of rain,
when we are far enough away to see.

2021

Early, Near the Courts

Cities in their waking slant sunshine into doorways,
bridge breakfast over morning into work.
Heartbreak finds its level, then silence.

Shadows on shop-fronts spill coffee into mortar.
Harsh-vowelled moments tie bows into brows,
co-accused and their mams smoking straight stories bent.

Clouds make a little dance above it all.

Freeport

Mandalas of dead crabs bloom on the sands
to sign off unspoken deals, the grift and graft
of two hundred years burning to an end.

What was found in the earth dissolved,
settled to sludge, slept unseen, waited.
We cut it, dredged what was, when all's said, ours.

The eels came first, a dead shine
we knew was not natural, inevitable or whole.
The auger pushed us into tomorrow.

Footsteps on the beach we must all approach:
a Crusoe's trail hidden in fret and fear,
lawyers' threats and official silence.

Flags warn you off the darkening water.
The breakers fill with stolen wealth, stones
glittering now but dull as clay at home.

The turbines wave and watch and are not heeded.
We live by the comings and goings of
such long-term contracts as the sea will hold.

They talk only about last night, what they did and

set free from the old grammar of *he said she said*
the words float, one minute secure in their antique
suggestions, the next replete only with possibility.
A finger traced a name on a thigh, but whose?

This is evolution in action, something
invisible until motion-captured, sped-up.
We should enjoy the feeling. Lean into it.
We do not have to specify everything.

Keep up. Calm down. You might feel lost
but the raw/cooked asymmetries will not work
as we move through this next passage of time.
I could say more, but I have finally caught on:

exegesis is a fingerprint, our only hope
the unknown, unlearnt, enamoured.

All communities are imagined communities:

desire paths across the council grasses,
muck on the wrong shoes we came out in, weather
to come unthought of, dog-walking neighbours
similarly overtaken by world and word.
The private whispers its smooth lexicon
into the readied ear. The sandbanks accrete
the rubble of demolition, hills of
concrete, a half century of rote learning.

As night gathers in the road, we tap out notes
on phones and wonder why we cannot sleep.
Restlessness demands a quiet story,
the old favourite where love and fear
wrestle for our desperate affections.
We are many, reading ourselves together.

New Year's Eve

The dogs are barking out the old year,
a squall of yelps and sputtering cries.
Another round of fireworks drums on,
inconclusively loud.
Paper thrown onto the coals
crumples like this last night.

There is fire burning elsewhere,
where the New Year always comes first.
The dogs there hide in damp bushes,
or stowaway in boat bottoms
as their families take to the lakes
to escape the flames of their towns.

Something is beginning.
Our dogs are barking out the old year.

Water

The thing we grow is not the thing we need.
The thing we need is the thing we pay for with the thing we grow.

We can wash it all away with water.
We can drown it or starve it, save it or kill it with water.

China grows its soya in Brazil to save water.
Why water when you can buy?

Why swim when you can pay a man pennies
to pour water from a bucket onto you all day?

This landscape is no longer ours, we need not irrigate it.
We can boil our eggs elsewhere.

Onions in Maharashtra may be Egyptian.
This year their own have too much water.

Water, like the future, is everywhere,
only unevenly distributed.

Policy Announcement

We say the same things again and again.
We set out today new resolutions.
We cannot just save the world: it must change.
We have mapped every consequence.
We know the value of the human heart.
We take no road but the road of courage.

We take no road but the road of courage.
We say the same things again and again.
We know the value of the human heart.
We set out today new resolutions.
We have mapped every consequence.
We cannot just save the world: it must change.

We cannot just save the world: it must change.
We take no road but the road of courage.
We have mapped every consequence.
We say the same things again and again.
We set out today new resolutions.
We know the value of the human heart.

We know the value of the human heart.
We cannot just save the world: it must change.
We set out today new resolutions.
We take no road but the road of courage.
We say the same things again and again.
We have mapped every consequence.

We have mapped every consequence.
We know the value of the human heart.
We say the same things again and again.
We cannot just save the world: it must change.
We take no road but the road of courage.
We set out today new resolutions.

We set out today new resolutions.
We have mapped every consequence.
We take no road but the road of courage.
We know the value of the human heart.
We cannot just save the world: it must change.
We say the same things again and again.

Forgotten resolutions clog the heart,
their consequences a cleft of change,
courage cracked open, again.

Technique

for Tin Arts

'Without recourse to lying, distortion or cheating. Technique!'
                                                    Prefab Sprout

If every step, leap, joke, twist and turn
became talk's straight opposite, a way
of being and doing, a chance to learn
what our bodies could shut up and say,

how fair it could be, this love-studded world,
how much more just and beautiful,
if every day new expressions unfurled
and we were all present in the impossible.

When you practice the art of listening
you never walk into the same room twice.
You find what the yet to be formed can bring.
You understand no single language can suffice.

Decades of readiness now, choices made,
dots joined without anomaly,
yet there are still fresh games to be played:
connections, laughter, lives, family.

To dream of tin means to open your mind,
your chest, your arms, your lungs, your heart,
and to stay open, ready to find
what the imagination can only ever start.

It is a gift you learn over time by giving,
the ancient grace and art of how to fall,
to hold your weight new and now and living,
until time slips loose the body's call:

instincts turn to muscled curiosity,
fluent patterns deliberate on balance,
a tight-held hint of what could be
were we fully ourselves and with others could dance.

We can all flow further, higher, and then…
It is what it becomes. We are where we are.
Gravity loses. We begin again.
Technique takes the weight, burns it to a star.

Anniversary Aubade

We contemplate the outside world,
the dawn chorus's tight crackle.
Sun edges in around the blinds.
The clocks that twitched us out of dreams
joke about the waiting morning,
massing hours of work and duty,
that rivered life not far away:
limitless, exhausting, ours.

The warmth that kept us sleeping holds.
A guttered spark that flares again.
Eight dry thoughtless minutes pass.
The tale runs on beyond us now.
Ten thousand times or more we have
woken in this way. Not yet enough.

Homewards

'That England is populated will always come as a surprise; humans can live on an island only by forgetting what an island represents.'

Gilles Deleuze

'I had never handled a tool in my life; and yet, in time, by labour, application, and contrivance, I found at last that I wanted nothing but I could have made it, especially if I had had tools.'

Daniel Defoe,
Robinson Crusoe

Misunderstandings

The dark is sitting in me.
This house lives in us.
The newspapers read our worries.
The bad news is full of our dreams.

What is to come watches me and shivers.
Words contain me.
Hours spend themselves playing me music.
My eyes close me down.

Breath takes me in.
Breath takes me in.
It feels me calm.

Now I am watching the dark.
I will wait until it sleeps
then slip away.

The Minister is Dreaming in the Sun

A man is knocking down a high brick wall
to rebuild it further from the swollen river,
each brick re-finds its original neighbour,
the wall somehow more massive than before.

Torrential rain from a bright sky,
though the ground is bone.
Days of rain upon the man and the wall in minutes
make him pace back and forth and change tack.

Now he is smashing the bricks, bagging the bits,
piling the bags in a line, then a stack, then, well, a wall.
The water laps against the bags, soaks them dull.
The earth is a footprint set hard and sharp.

There are children up on roofs, arms out,
shadowing helicopters and planes,
smudge-faced children down in the dirt
scratching for tools of make believe.

There are parents looking for their children,
good parents looking for naughty and nice alike.
The motives of others, says the voiceover,
the unfathomable motives of others.

Freedom

We are not to be distracted or negotiated with.
We are settled in our utility.

If you have come here to broaden our minds,
with your questions and your silence doing the work,

You will feel something you did not expect.
You will carry away the marks on your skin.

What did you think we were going to say?
Look at us. Look around you. This is it,

my friend, the point you turn around,
go home to spread the word of our welcome.

We want to share it with everyone.
We want to teach the world our ways.

We are done with being alone.
We are done with being alone.

Borders

1

It is the night, and I am being patient.
It is the night, and I am being patient.
The knock of the hour a tick in my ear -
it is the night, and I am being patient.

This is the very least of it, of course,
but though the day keeps you invisible
with its meetings and emails and mithering,
you have calmly settled in my dreams
like a man into the next seat on the train
and now it is the night and I am being patient.

2

I dream of gulls, of fog over water,
waves without status slowing and gone,
paddles lost on paid-for seas.
I am wrapped up safe and silent.
You are done with being afraid,
would rather the long crossing
into my dreams, that small house
in my head where furniture steams
as the hot night sets me twitching.
Where a calm man counts his fingers,
looks us in the eye and says how much
he wants to welcome all in need
of welcome, all so tirelessly working
to escape this fidgeting century.
He wants to share his ways,
and you, you are the start of that.

All around the edge of the room
sit a host of anxious faces,
wide-awake backs to cold walls.
They want their horizons wider,
their borders buttered on both sides.

Festival

Tents ploughed into furrows unfurl beneath rainy squalls.
Pegs glisten into folds of shirts, pants, a small shoe.
This field is home only to hope, not optimism.
Whatever release is sought in this camp's sour air
may not come, but it makes sense. Rain and sun,
self-generating dirt, will fallow these tents whole again.
Little by little their corners and curves will surface,
and as farmers pull back the flaps, caution tight within them,
a parade of geese will burst out and head for home,
wintering dark scratches into the sky. No other trace.

Such fresh wilderness as this will leave will miss them.
The forsaken tents will rot back into the fields,
with the shattered tibia and fibula, femurs and hips,
the chipped skulls of all our other wars.

***

And we shall make this city not from egg boxes
but from egg shells we have walked into dust,
not from bricks and mission statements but from
cold morning-after chips scattered like dandruff,
panic-sweat boiled down to mortar, not clean
engineered realisations but scratches, scrawls,
sprawls of forks stuck in dirt, from blood.

***

They walked away from home
and the birds and clouds shadowed them,
birds like clouds and clouds like drones
spread in the hover, lines over steps,
steps tracing platforms, quaysides,
railways, roadstops, ditches,
heartless powerlines queueing
the wrong sides of borders.

The lights are the lights of boats
that flash as they move and dig
rushing tunnels through water,
then harbour away in the dark
where the lights keep all afloat,
string the shortest ticks of hope
into song and signal.

None of them the moon,
the moon all dream of,
all hope glowing for the moon
that the lights cannot be
till tide brings them home
far from home, nowhere next,
a pause alone, staring at
the lights, the lights of boats.

Homewards

The sea so far away seeming, always,
beyond sands clagged to wind-carved dunes,
slack salted with marram, wort and worry.

Waves arrive from who knows where,
the flat edge of the unknown slipped
beneath our door, a last note unfound

whose words spread to let roots cling.
Thrift gathers marbled bells of red and pink,
strung out for the wind to chime.

The oceans did not need to rise,
left us what once we worked so hard.
All gone to mud and dry now,

to someday crack, water rivering
into new lakes, slopes and knolls,
villages creeping solidly downhill.

So far from sea and nowhere, still.
A simple place to live, a stack
of logs set to dry for burning,

a fire for ache and tired talk,
miraculously strange tongues
made powerful by company,

the craft of our walking and talking
a place into being, our only home
the hearth of the yards ahead of us.

And if we do not meet again

remember how I could fold birds from paper,
hands a blur inside the story of a house,
our old house growing old by a garden full of trees
branched with birds and sunlight only days ago, only hours.

Remember how I would bite my lip to stillness
when father called me faithless, faceless, lost,
how I screwed down tears to prove myself
not dreamless despite all, not flightless.

If we do not meet again remember my hands,
how they would pause as if frozen in my thought
then skitter to rest again on my chest

as I explained our journey, the road and seas
winding back to my beginning, every knuckle crack
a hard crumb dropped to tell the way back home.

For Some People in a House Without Walls

Where once beneath the stairs you folded
your arms around your knees, the dusty air
holding you together, now you are
open, breathless, bare.

A home without walls: no distance, no dance
but the wind shaking the shadow of your coat
for attention, to give some lasting point
to the sentence you cannot finish.

Here there is no hearth, no heart, no song.
In the quiet you make an endless list
of new guidance on how to be with others,
how to rhyme your silence with theirs.

You wake from dreams of holiday breakfasts
as a child, tiny under blankets crunching apples.
Where you are now, your phone never rings.
And yet the day somehow seems to begin.

They think they are the serious ones but

they treat each day as a game. They do not know
the cardboard smell inside cupboards,
the shaving of shredded wheat, the tang of
hunger that dehydrates in a moment,
sends you early to bed, early to rise,
and never shares, never passes the bread.
Their game is called Going Without Pudding.
You play yours in the dark when data runs out.
You play it when you walk around the block.
You play it when you carve little holes in
the hard skin that forms around your heels.
You walk and you walk and do not go without,
you play game after game of Hungry Revenge
all the way home, all the way home, all the way home.

The Present Imperfect

an improvisation on Yves Bonnefoy's 'L'imperfection est la cime'

A need to stop and stop and stop,
to save ourselves, only that, cheap at any price.

We spoil the new face that emerges
from the marble, hammer any grace, any beauty.

We'd love that perfect thing a wide-opened door,
But deny it as soon as we saw it, look away.

The present imperfect is now our summit.

If We Look Back

two channel stereo

our pockets will empty
the morning will appear
suitcases will fall into mud
fingers will let slip their hold
the soles of our shoes will burn
coins will rattle beneath our feet
rain will etch refusal on our cheeks
our unforgotten gardens will crumble
all telephones will start ringing at once
the stinging behind our eyes will spread
all joints will double and ache in the damp
turrets and guns will shadow our every step
ground will shake as a tank accompanies us
hems of dresses will fray like flags in the wind
seconds will slow until they hardly fill our lungs
our fists will close and cramp to drive into walls
a sudden bitterness of violets will fill the sharp air
the timid amongst us will lift their voices and sing
fences will surround our nostalgia and hold it back
words will fly from our mouths in tongueless music
DNA will unravel land-bound helixes to mimic seas
the pages of last books will unbind themselves and fly
the photos next to our hearts will fade to white of skies
the skies grown ever hotter at the hard hollow heart of us
until we put our hands on scalding earth and with it we weep

There'll be nothing but photos to look at, a timeline of what
we wanted to be, how we needed it to appear. Cliché will
become a safe house where we can laugh when dark has
to be forgotten. We will throw away all our diaries and
albums, rely on the security of clouds until rains come
and stay forever. Not bad people, we will not drown.
Holding the kids' hands we'll look from bedrooms
onto the hi-viz panic, wonder who was helping us,
who among us was guilty. We are not so shallow
we won't wonder if it was us, dry tinder inside,
seeing what happened next as just whatever
happened next. Something natural. Baked
in. We will forgive ourselves our lives
even as they slide free of everything.
Our ghosted past will hold on only
to our dreams, those forlorn skins
sloughed off each drop-dead
night, memories crumbling
like icebergs. Chunk by
still cold chunk. We
will leave. We will
leave all we had
before. Before
we had to
wake.

Moving the Books

We are moving the books again,
the hard-working books.
We are piling them in our arms,
the ones we want to save.
We are carrying them up the stairs
into the now spare room.
We are stacking them carefully
in now sentimental spaces.
If one comes in one must go out.
We are full. The house is full.
But still, we are moving the books,
to maintain order and beauty.
We share our home with these ideas.
They will reward us for our efforts.

This is the reward for our efforts.
We share our home with this idea:
that we can maintain order and beauty.
Even though we have moved the books
we are full. The house is full.
If one comes in one must go out.
There are no sentimental spaces.
We bring them back carefully
from the now spare room.
We carry them down the stairs,
the ones we cannot save.
We hold them piled in our arms,
the exhausted books we do not want.
We have been moving the books again.

A Confession

'Smell comes before volatiles created by chewing, that then combine in throat and nose to make taste. Taste is thus an act of triangulation.'

Carolyn Steel

Born backwards, October 1964

An unsure arrival:
not in the /b/ of boom
but the outbreath /m/,
a sigh no bigger
than a spoonful of syrup,
a stifled cough, a spasm
disguised inside an air
that twists its tight-lipped
hard-stopped beginning
round to a familiar tune:

O mother where art thou?
O mother where did the time go?
O mother what now?
O mother join in my song.

1970

I imagine the boy not yet six,
in shorts, stepping out of a pedal car.
He goes in the back way, off the drive,
through the kitchen, slides the lounge doors
apart and Dad puts the telly on.
The yellow shirts play the blue shirts,
Pele and his pals magicking.

He goes out and the estate is still being built.
It's all paled out by the summers to come.
He steps over the footprint the cat left
while the drive was drying.
By the end of the cul-de-sac
he has taken his A levels
and is packing his bags.

It's as simple and quick as that,
but it happens again and again.
He is like a tennis ball rallied
against the side of the house.
The fence he broke stick by stick
with his leather cricket ball
still smells of creosote behind him.

'Kin Errors:

a Künstlerroman in 18 years, after Raymond Queneau's 'Un Beau Siècle'

Stupidity of 1964,
midwife telling my parents to
switch my names around
to confuse doctors and dentists
Bullshit of the sixties, man,
late issues of Oz hidden in the attic
as the estate filled up around them
Bullshit of the seventies,
being good at school
Idiocy of '72,
dad taking redundancy from Courtauld's
so we could buy a colour telly
to watch Sweet on Top of the Pops
Bullshit of the long-middle seventies,
rationing of candles for our own good
Bullshit of '76,
11+ pass + posh shop uniform list
= x, therefore y =
a cardboard briefcase from BHS
Bullshit of two sevens clashing,
horizons dark with fake leather jackets
Bullshit of 1979,
crisis what crisis o that crisis gathering itself
Bullshit of 1980,
President's day at the Con Club under duress

Bullshit of the eighties,
walking home from the Warehouse
hoping for a lift from a Menzies van
that didn't pass through the Falklands
Penultimate bollocks of summer '83,
the regrettable incidents of A level result day
Climactic Bullshit of 1983,
the tutor asking 'Does your accent
get stronger when you've had a drink?'

Self-portrait discovered while playing with two triangles by Guillevic

1.

I have succeeded in establishing
a little order within myself.

I like to feel pleased.

2.

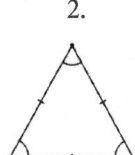

I have gone too far
with my concern for order.

Nothing else is allowed to happen.

1= Isosceles Triangle
2 = Equilateral Triangle

DNA tells me

no more than the mirror.
Lots of cold Lancastrian sky,
clouds blown in from Ireland
or down from Scotland.
A butter pie where my heart
should be. Maybe next time
I'll sparkle, but for now
I enjoy the plainness,
the unobjectified life
of the spud-faced obvious
that returns my gaze,
wondering just who the hell
I think I am.

The mice in the attic

have shredded the literary archive
stuffed in boxes at the back of the eaves –
all those hard-won early works.

Thank the good lord Mulch.
May they make for dry homes.

A Confession

My friends, I left my foot in and I followed through.
I ploughed on when pace left me for dead.
I pulled out of simple 50:50s.
I chose when to stand still and become
something hard to bounce off.
I made bad decisions and I saw passes
my limbs could not thread in a month.
I took my eye off the ball and I ball-watched.
I got caught in two minds.
I picked up the banjo but could not hit the barn door.
I asked too much of tired legs, shot from distance,
failed to make sure of anything much.
I may have led with my elbow,
I certainly stuck out my chin and leant in.

I dreamt, my friends, I dreamt of a better world.

Tasting Menu

1. Onion

In the beginning was the word and the word
was onion. Babylon dried it for hard times,
quenched thirst that guaranteed eternal life,
globes for mummified kings to chew on.

Dad sliced it into vinegar: spiked crescents
browning in malt, adding their own bite
to keep us somehow unpoisoned by the chicken
kept in the cupboard Sunday to Wednesday.

Life taught me that the onion powers us all,
succour and bitterness combined,
more valuable than money or water –
sharper, fresher. It is an anger firing up.

Yet I also know you cannot be angry
chopping onions with a freshly sharp knife.

2. Salt

Salt makes neither adjectives nor adverbs
but syntax, parched intensity that expands
and connects everything it touches, until
not enough is too much, evidence
Epicurus was right that nothing is enough
for the person for whom enough is too little.

Salt exaggerates its way through life,
appears from the damp it absorbs.
It was once common sense, the everyday
that proved the world could be trusted,
we can be human and careful even
as the seas pressure us for decisions.
The heart still races when we taste it.
It knows who and what will last.

3. Pepper

A projection of the meeting of seed and fruit,
an exchange of sun and heat, flowering vines
caught as spikes to dry and turn to trade.

How resolute between the fingers,
that hint of temper beneath the smile,
choler and fret resolved by a look
full in the eye, the paying of respect.

A dance on the tongue, the back of the nose
and into the eyes, the tear ducts, the
 – hold it, hold it, hold it –
mythical sneeze you wanted as a child
but never achieved, no matter how much you snuffed.

This is the fire that deigns not to declare itself,
but wraps its strength in silence.

4. Radish

> *'When radishes aren't good enough, pretty soon nothing is good enough.'*
> Edward Espe Brown

> *'In Minneapolis the food coops fought each other with papers with titles such as 'On the Radish Threat to the Process of Dialectical Self-Interpretation in the Co-Op Movement: A Coughing Spasm'.'*
> Jonathan Kaufmann

We will eat these quickly, hotly, carve them
into statues of our granddads in cardigans
on the fabled Night of the Radishes,
a festival stolen from Mexico
to celebrate or undermine our appetite.
We will choke on our French Breakfasts
and White Icicles, our April Crosses
and our giant daikon and mooli
before we abandon our ideals.
We will pluck them and have them eaten
by the time we reach the kitchen.
These small luxuries will be the bonus
to our salary of onions and garlic,
temptation to warm us through the winter.

5. Tofu

Substance given to nothing, or almost
nothing, net result of mash and water.
A challenge of addition and extraction
until flavour accumulates.

As white as a turnip or the moon
but with no bite, no bite at all,
just a yielding to the rain.
And yet there is a skin

waiting to harden in the heat,
a depth ready to soak up the salty dark
of its fermented cousins,
opposite branch of the family tree.

All from the ground, from the ground
and water, time, impatience.

6. Brown Rice

> *'When you wash the rice, wash the rice.'*
> Suzuki Roshi, quoted by Edward Espe Brown

When you wash the rice, wash the rice.
Stay with the chill in your fingers a minute.

Let the grains end as they start, in water's flow.
If you are still hungry it will fill you,

let you sleep if you have cooked it well.
A tight lid is best, just a thumb's worth

of water, maybe half in California
where draught bakes farmers into attention

to every grain, to shrinking wetlands, each
irrigated inundation, every bowl

sweeter and fatter than they grew up with.
Do not think about it while it boils. Trust

the process, the opening of the heart.
Those worlds inside the bran cannot be rushed.

7. Custard

I don't want to write a poem
about my Nan Nelson's custards,
sunlight refracted by yellowed milk,
the simple breakfast bowl she baked in,
how nutmeg's middle notes went flying
past the shed outside the window,
its tarred skin just starting to fray,
beyond it the hedged run along the garden
by the peas and beans and rhubarb:
all that much closer to wartime than we thought.

I don't want to suggest these memories
are more than something for you to complete.

If you are out there, dear reader, my mirror,
accept this poor apology for a pudding.

My father died a year ago today

and ever since I have run with a pain
that slipped into my gut to slow me down,
that tugs me into standing still, into
stretching, into watching in the mirror
the weakened walls of my belly extend
into ridges of a new self pushing
reluctantly through to be born, a tear,
while my mind spins and the daily routines
of work and world and woe rotate in time
with loss, with shouts and silences, the rests
and crescendos, the hills, plains, descents
the call-less year has ground into my knees.
The breath that says I am still here I am
still here I am still here I am still here.

***

Along the railway path, toward the mile mark,
I see my dad looking out from Coach A
of the 6.15 Transpennine Express,
a half-read murder open before him.
He looks straight through me. This is not right.
He has not boarded a train since 19-
77 when he and Scouse Tiny
(6 foot eight) went to the League Cup Final,
leaving their wives to souvenir pencils
and dodgy watches from Portobello Road.
I stop, let the sunset varnish the wound
whose cracked crust reflects his gaze even now.
I stretch my hamstrings before I set off again,
my body knowing more than my mind remembers.

***

Cooling down up the backs from Harry's Shop
as I near home, Al's car's on the hard standing.
He rounds the corner on his mobility
scooter, waving a bag of giant cream cakes,
laughing at my raised eyebrows, the furrows
his enthusiasm carves in my doubt.
He said not even death could keep him from
the cake shop, from putting right the people
who park on pavements so he cannot cross.
He approaches, waving again, clocking me,
my breathlessness and silence.
I want to make him a brew, I want to
help him sit down and turn the telly on,
but by the time my breath has eased he's gone.

***

Running the Tees in trail shoes I am dredged-
up, just the one idea left to me:
rhythm trumps pain. But I have forgotten
how swollen tides spill over into pools,
how pools deepen into ponds, brooks, streams –
until the path finds itself all river.
As I trudge back to the car I see him
in the passenger seat of a Micra
facing a murmuration, dusk dimming
to lightless variations on the dark.
The space between cars is tight, seems to
narrow as I squeeze in. He looks right at me.
He gives me a nod, points at the starlings'
improvised choreography. We drive away.

(The title of this poem is an echo of the opening line from *No Time to Cry* by Iris Dement, in a failed attempt to get it out of my head.)

Attempting to Leave

He locked the door, turned round and walked off down
the street towards the park. He turned around,
walked back to the door and turned the handle.
He felt a slow satisfying jarring in his wrist.
He locked the door, walked back to his car
and got in. He turned the engine on and
listened carefully to its low rumble for
two whole minutes. Then he got out, walked back
to the house holding his breath, got his keys
out of his pocket dramatically,
then opened and closed the door as if
he had forgotten what he'd gone back for.
He ran to the car as if hurrying.
As he began to ease away, he changed
his mind, braked, jumped out, keys dangling in
the ignition, the door open slightly.
He jogged back down the path, swinging his arms.
He opened the door, stooped to pick something
invisible from the mat. He tutted
in a stage whisper and locked up again.
He backed away into empty space,

a new stanza,

then another,

before a last check nothing was open.

In a different light

we could be people from another side of town,
either end of the long main road.
One end I'd likely be near dead now,
the other I'm talked of as young, fit.
I just need a better haircut, to lose
a few pounds, or to take up carelessness.
Our nightly cost-benefit analysis
remains undecisive, ambiguous:
bright when we first pick it up, dull the next.
It's nostalgia we're feeling, not panic,
a chord delayed from the ringing moment
we made our choice, a modulation
we had forgotten would track us down.
We like it, it sounds like something new,
But it is becoming deafening.

One time we hired a bouncy castle
off a man with a van and a pump.
It was one of the kids' birthdays.
For reasons I can't remember or ask
it was put it in the front room.
It grew and grew, slowly, in fits, twitches,
sudden standings to attention.
It filled the alcoves and the bay.
The rhythmic wheeze of its expansion
subsided into creaks and hisses.
The kids squeezed in and bounced madly.
Had we moved everything out?
I suppose we must have done.

Well, that bouncy castle, that room,
that creaking and panting,
that explosion that never came,
no matter how hard they all jumped?

That's the tinnitus I secretly cherish now.

Some days

his cheek bones appear out of nowhere,
greeted with surprise by the lines under
and around his eyes. He holds in his belly.

His dreams are full of cooch grass,
long white strands under the surface
that shock him with their resilience.

Running across the forecourt
on the corner, blown-in seagulls
swoop down and mock his aspirations.

He just wants to be a little more flexible.
He just wants half an hour to read a book.
He just wants the shadow of a tree to fall on him.

A Message From the Recently Dead

I know even my life was too long
to transcribe at normal speed
but if you run this world faster
than the pace of its happening
you shorten only the afterlife.
The conversation was rarely as
urgent as all that, was it?
Let us take a second.
Let us all just take a second.

Epithalamium for Cineastes

Not the lion roaring, or hammered gong,
nor the turning earth illuminating,
or playful Anglepoise sick of waiting –
open cold in heated flashback: a song.

Withhold the actual moment of marriage.
Hide for repeat viewing secrets in plain sight,
two frames cut together by magic light,
golden-houred confidence trick of courage

conspiring to kern characters, hearts,
joined by what they each find in the other,
a fresh edit they now make together,
a wonderful life of surprises and starts.

Two we love break the fourth wall with a glance.
They address us: we are ready to dance.

Recursion

'I think it is true that one gains a certain hold on sausage and haddock by writing them down.'

Virginia Woolf,
8 March 1941

Recursion: a mobile rendered in two dimensions

Such fresh wilderness as this
the house of bark, bite and bitterness
the house of rain and regret

> Morning drags shadows across the garage
> the apple tree walking away
> the cherries' tiny bulbs of reddening pink
> flash dot and dash as if to say
> 'Help us. We are being held captive.'

>> Mud-stuck
>>
>> with just the one idea left:
>> how the river's flow could strike you dumb
>> with its sunlit opposition
>> to the coldness of radiators and bathroom tiles
>>
>> the lightless yard through the window
>> next door watching through the fence
>> the kitchen clock ticking, kicking
>> a slow turn into a drum beat
>>
>> a smudged dance down to nothing

A thread of hope traced
back to the source
taken as a cutting

                Guttering scrapes of adoration

        A shed of slats and iron drowns
        in ferns
        in comfrey
        that will power the spring

Wind upturned the elder and still it grows
hosts on its perpendicular face
a world of blooms to tap
into the fungal constellations below

        There is no need
        for the sound bed of birds
        between front door and station
        the murmuration of whistles
        and loops a conversation
        to start the day
        no need at all

The morning tracks us down all by itself
It poses no questions
asks us for nothing

> The air is fragile with folk booking assistance
> for their journeys, smiling people in uniform
> will wait for them with ramps or simply
> a steady forearm a welcome

>> Yet my heart is in fog
>> fog over water
>> waves without status
>> slowing and gone
>> loosed from moorings
>> lost on their way home

From what beautiful and daft things have you turned away?

If all of this is spelt by stars
what worlds and universes
could you have embraced or fled to
if you had been brave enough?

The future is warm, small
growing out of dry dirt
The pleasures that made us
now catch in our throats

    Have you noticed how we're not
    getting any younger?

    The blue sky makes a scratch
    of something new
    enclosed days
    nights of twitching

    The air is syrup
    the air is mulch
    We may not age but
    it's now or never
    We're not getting any younger

        The fields are nearly full now
        of houses, water, lost pink lands
        on maps, guts and gas

Whatever grows here stays here

Tomorrow's a roadblock we cannot jump
The dusk we built up to is broken
Sing that old song anyway
The one about here and now

>The sound of the sea is the action
>The water is in and over the wheels
>The moon is turning the waves
>turning the days, turning the hours
>The drive home a line of stars

A fat man crosses the road
while the lights are green
He slows the traffic to a crawl
He holds onto the bumper
of a van for a minute before falling

>Gulls blown inland up river
>watch and swing to catch
>the bread thrown for them

Hope evaporates into the morning
segmented characteristics denied
when we see each other in the street

    Not the book in his hand
    nor the package it came in
    not the knock on the door
    nor the light on the roof of the van
    dazzling the man looking out his attic room
    window opened flat as if for cleaning
    but still patterned with dirt

        Not the sky calming the flashing lights
        like paper covers rock
        but the words

I dream of the dead and of those persisting

    We are all on board
    to stick with it
    We got this way
    through muscle and guile

Kin Errors' started with varying the terms used to translate the word 'Conneries' in the poem 'Un Beau Siècle' by Raymond Queneau in *Hitting the Streets* (Carcanet), translated by Rachel Galvin.

'Self-portrait discovered while playing with two triangles by Guillevic' puts together variations of two shape poems by Guillevic in the Gallimard *Anthologie de la poésie française du XXe siècle*. That is also where I discovered the poem by Yves Bonnefoy which I adapted in 'The Present Imperfect'. My poem was published by Bill Herbert and Andy Jackson's *New Boots and Pantisocracies* site in its *Postcards from Malthusia* series.

'A Confession' was first published by *And Other Poems*. The poem is dedicated to Andy Croft and the Dynamo Meths alumni.

The epigraph to 'Tasting Menu' comes from *Sitopia: How Food Can Save The World* by Carolyn Steele (Vintage Books). The epigraphs to 'Brown Rice' come from Jonathan Kaufmann's *Hippie Food* (William Morrow) and Edward Espe Brown's *Tomato Blessing and Radish Teachings* (Riverhead Books).

'Epithalamium for Cineastes' was written for Lou Robinson and Hannah Newman-Smart and first performed at Rich Mix, London, a few minutes after they had got married.

The epigraph to 'Recursion' is one of the final entries in Virginia Woolf's diaries.

The epigraphs from Gilles Deleuze are from the essay 'Desert Islands', translated by Michael Taormina (Semiotext(e)). I am grateful for the keynote speech at the World Summit for Arts and Culture in Johannesburg in 2009 by the then Slovenian Minister of Culture, Stojan Pelko, that alerted me to it.

Notes and acknowledgements

'The Infinite Town' was commissioned by Stockton-on-Tees Borough Council. Thanks to Reuben Kench. If you're ever in Stockton at 1pm, you can read it as an animatronic train made by artist Rob Higgs emerges, hooting and steaming.

'From the Proverbs of Aurora Boroborealis' was commissioned by Stellar Projects for the Nightfall Festival in 2022. Thanks to Rachel Willis and Lyndsey Stephenson for their support, and to Gijs Van Bon for his Nyx machine which printed out the Proverbs in light emitting sand along the paths of Stewarts Park in Middlesbrough. Hindsight was commissioned by Stellar Projects for the Nightfall Festival in 2021.

'The disappearing men' and 'Attempting to Leave' were first published in *Masculinity: An anthology of modern voices* (Broken Sleep), edited by Rick Dove, Aaron Kent, and Stuart McPherson.

'All communities are imagined communities' adapts a phrase of Benedict Anderson, in *Imagined Communities* (Verso).

'Technique' was commissioned by Tin Arts dance company of County Durham to mark their 20th birthday and is dedicated to Tess Chaytor and Martin Wilson.

'The Minister is Dreaming in the Sun' was first published in *New Boots and Pantisocracies* (Smokestack Books), edited by WN Herbert and Andy Jackson.

'Freedom' was first published by Visual Verse.

'Homewards' was first published in *The Long White Thread of Words: poems for John Berger* (Smokestack Books), edited by Amarjit Chandan, Gareth Evans and Yasmin Gunaratnam.

Voices thrown where river bends

The brick pond where photographers gather
for the murmuration – their own peeling
into a queue at the roundabout
an echoed dance
freedom turned to constraint

    Broken branches slow-snagged
    on the unfinished tide
    the too smooth sound of news radio
    If it is what it takes
    this is where I shall let go

        And so the retraining begins
        The street scene seen innocently
        innocently senses its demise
        The terraced streets shrug off
        the flashbacks and feel new

          This is this
          this is

This is not the morning of the century

Infinite clouds pour rain in the distance
pencil shading of some stubborn talent

>Forgive us
>>the half empty car parks
>>the stubble fields
>>the caravans lost
>>to mould and bushes
>>the new builds
>>the bridges
>>the COVID LIES graffiti
>>the shuttered mini retail parks
>>the piles of cars
>>the rotting white vans
>>the dogs on chains
>>the cathedrals and conversions
>>the money pits
>>the flaking conservatories
>>the choreographed jobs
>>the pining commuter park and rides
>>the terraces abandoned to HMOs
>>the optimistic set of solar panels
>>the beckoning platform edge
>>the yellow lines
>>the trees on the right side of the tracks
>>the goal posts wide open white and rusty

Lights out in the industrial kindergartens
the wheezing enterprise zone, whole
exhausted landscapes bitten chunk by chunk
by chunk to dark

>Parents pull small children from their car seats
>jolly them into Reception and Year One
>smooth over the separation tears, flatten collars
>The teachers are already tired though
>There is simply not enough coffee in the world

>>We are writing letters, clicking like
>>pointing out the comments, our contempt
>>We are wailing silently into our phones
>>Trains run as on time as ever though
>>The fields by the track flood and vanish

This island, undeserved home
of those who made it here, unmade
by nostalgic dreams undreamt,
spoilt from spite at the unspoilt spit
and polish of the unpolished blow-ins

>What was done must be undone

The skies tie themselves in knots
around hacked off branches of the family tree

> Some people have light inside them
> the inevitable unwilled light
> of a solar lamp stuck into the edge
> of a tired peri-urban lawn, full of only
> time, only time, that passes, is shared
> and then turns to the invisible

>> I too have turned invisible
>> so much the aged standard
>> I can do what I like
>> Perhaps this has always been so:
>> I just did not know

Our photos in our hands, always
Our hands always ready, always
open to receive what the day decides
Today decided to say go
do not collect, do not look
do not hesitate, mean what you mean
mean what you mean

> The photos in our hands
> those beloved faces and skies
> glimpsed between calls on trains
> those beloved faces will wait and see
> will wait and watch

I dream of a week of sleep
I sleep like a stone on a riverbed

        I am still too heavy
        But I am not so too heavy
        As I used to be

        Pride goes to fall

Come Sunday fortnight
this will all be over
the wind will drop
the swell of horns diminuendo
rest for the weary

    Asleep in the simple room
    a dream happens itself awake
    Your mind thins out fresh shoots
    Bird chatter rattles the Velux

    You work out how many breakfasts
    this table has sat through with you
    Spring nudges at the door
    in the shape of a young cat

The morning is exactly here
The shadow of the apple tree examines the garage wall
The breath you took remade itself
Tomorrow waits in the backs

    Not that person on a bench waiting
    to be listened to as they imagine
    a warmer afternoon than
    exactly now
    exactly here
    their clothes a sketch of lines
    that skitter away like steam

        This is the place we all reach:
        a threshold hidden in sand and sea
        where winds push you out of riptides
        not caring if what comes next is
        a secret or a mystery
        unafraid

Do unto others is advice for angels
not human beings
but there are no angels to hear it
only human beings